Letters

From

Your Fathers

Things We Want You to Know

BRIAN HENDERSON

-WITH-

Anthony Hailstock,

Jamal Hasan, Travis Valentine,

& Demario Mattox

Letters

From Your

Fathers

Things We Want You to Know Volume One

BRIAN HENDERSON

FEATURING

ANTHONY HAILSTOCK, JAMAL HASAN,
TRAVIS VALENTINE, & DEMARIO MATTOX

Volume One

ISBN: 9781659594652

This book is

dedicated to our children.

Our hope is that you understand

how deep our love goes

for you all!

CONTENTS

INTRODUCTION

WHAT YOU NEED TO KNOW

To: Our Children

From: Your Fathers

Re: What You Need to Know

Dear Sons and Daughters,

When you all came into this world, we want you to know that you changed our lives forever. A love filled our hearts that we had never before experienced. We have watched you grow and have celebrated each milestone you reached. From your first footsteps, to your first words, and even your first poop in the pot, we have been your biggest fans and cheerleaders. You have taught us just as much, if not more, than we could ever teach ourselves. However, there are some things we want you to know. There are some things you need to know. For some of us fathers, there are some things you deserve to know about how, when, and why you were born.

Some of us were ready for you, and some of us weren't. To be honest, some of you were an accident, or in other words, a slip-up. Regardless of how you were made, you all changed our lives in some shape, form, or fashion. For better or worse, you all are important pieces that made us better men.

You probably think we are the greatest fathers in the world. Some of us think we are, and some of us believe we could do better. You need us to be reliable. You need us to be responsible. You need us to be there for you since you can't be there for yourselves. However, many of us haven't always been who you needed us to be.

We weren't always there for you. Some of us weren't even there for your mothers during the nine months she carried you. Some of us had verbal fights with your moms, and sometimes we missed your doctor's appointments. Some of us were still in relationships with your mothers, and some of us were not. Regardless, we all should have been there as fathers, ensuring your delivery into this world was as smooth as possible. Fortunately, for many of you, your mothers were capable of bringing you into this world with or without our support.

You have to understand, we all aren't perfect. Our relationships weren't all smooth. Some of our transitions into a family were rough. Also, some of you didn't like us as fathers when you were born. This is why we wrote you these letters. You needed to hear from us how we felt bringing you into this world. You need to understand the many challenges and hurdles we had to overcome to become what you needed us to be. One day you will read these letters and hopefully gain insight into us, your fathers.

We fathers are definitely not all alike. We come from different backgrounds, have different personalities, and all were probably in different places in our lives. However, one thing is the same of each of the fathers that have written letters in this book. We all needed you in our lives. We all were missing you in our lives. We all are better because of you. We all thank you. Most importantly, we all love you!

1

CHAPTER ONE

DEAR BRAYLEN, BRI'ANN, AND BRAXTON

Dear Bray, Bri, and Brax,

Let me first say this: You have all taught me more about life than I could ever teach you. Up until you all came into this world, I always felt as if I was missing something. Any goal I had reached or success I gained, there was always a feeling that I was missing someone with me on my journey. While the puzzle of my life is still incomplete and will probably never be completed, you three are pieces that filled many voids I never knew I had.

After I graduated college, I thought I was living large. I could go wherever I wanted. I could date whomever I wanted. I could do whatever I wanted. I didn't truly understand what responsibilities were. I had no idea what true sacrifice meant. Time management was a whole new skill I had to learn. I also honestly never knew what true love was until I gazed upon each one of your beautiful eyes.

Braylen, you are my first born, my prince, and my oldest. You helped fill a void that I had in my life. I was always "Uncle B" to so many kids. You made your entrance into this world and transformed me into “Daddy.” During the first years of your life we were everywhere together, went everywhere together, and did everything together. I always dressed you like me, treating you like you were a mini-me. Even though you were your momma’s boy, you were also daddy’s little man. I have embraced that role more than anything else I have embraced in my life.

Being a father was a new challenge for me. I never experienced some of the struggles I gained from becoming your father. I’ve always seen and heard different dads express how much their lives changed once their children came into the world. Hearing, seeing, and then actually living it are all completely different. Things became real when I had to change your diaper, make your bottle, burp you, put you to sleep, bathe you, and many other responsibilities that came with the new title. While I shared these responsibilities with your mother, I felt as if I had to overdue things just because you were a little boy. I've always felt that a young boy needs his father!

Things became even tougher once your mom and I decided to split. It caused so much extra stress on you, and I could feel it. I could see it through your actions at school. I could hear it through the different things you would say or ask. I also experienced the unintentional rebelliousness you exhibited all because you were having tough times dealing with our reality. Our reality is now one of a blended family. You have both a step-mom and step-dad that love you dearly. We all are a big part of your village. This village will always make sure we put you first regardless of any differences we may have.

You are now eight years old and one of the most handsome, intuitive, and intelligent kids ever. You not only helped me embrace being a father, but you also made my thirst stronger for more. I wanted to share the bond we had with another, preferably with a little girl. I wanted you to have a little sister that we could both bond with. I wanted to see if I could be the father to a daughter, as you had helped me become a father to you, my first born, and my first son. As fate would have it, Bri'Ann would join us four years later.

Princess Bri'Ann, you totally shook up my world. When you first arrived, I loved you. However, our first week together, you frustrated me more than any other person had ever. You wouldn't let me feed you, hold you, burp you, bathe you, change you, or love you without crying. I doubted myself as a father. Your mother doubted the effort I was putting in with you. I remember her stating that I cared more about Braylen than you. That statement was far from the truth. You just honestly scared the hell out of me. I thought I could raise you just like I did Braylen. How quickly I found out, that wasn’t the case.

Your mother's questioning of my effort with you just happened to be the best thing that could've ever happened for us. I took her view of me with you as a challenge. You know I love a challenge. I remember making it my everyday goal to assure you that you were "Daddy's Girl." I had to give you extra time and attention, which allowed me to see the error of my ways.

I remember I was initially frustrated with the new challenges. First, I assumed I couldn't feed you because you were being nursed. Your mommy taught me how to overcome that obstacle by freezing her milk and showing me how to prepare it for you. After a while, you became comfortable with me feeding you. Then, I was upset because you only wanted to sleep with your mommy. I believe feeding you helped you finally allow yourself to be comfortable and lay on me, like your big brother used to. Finally, I became comfortable with changing you.

When I first changed you, your mommy was letting me have it. “You’re wiping too hard,” she said. “You can’t wipe that way. Go front to back.” I was completely terrified to touch you. Things got better, and I realized you were my baby girl, not my baby boy. I just had to toughen up and do my job.

Over the next few months, we became so close. You, Bray, and I would spend so much time together. I have thousands of pictures and hundreds of videos between your six-month age and when you turned one that highlight the bond we had begun to grow. I started to dress us alike, just as I had with Bray. We took our first road trip together with just you, Bray, and I to Philadelphia. We dressed like minions for Halloween. Now, I can't get rid of you, and I love it. You are my princess, my baby girl. You have shown us how tough and sassy you are. You definitely act like a big sister to Braylen. Not even two years would pass before you actually became a big sister, as the third little Henderson arrived.

Braxton, Braxton, Braxton! Let me be very honest with you. It took us two chances to make you. That's something most people don't know. However, I can speak for both your mommy and me when I say that the wait was well worth it. You are everything that we could ever imagine in being the youngest of the bunch. And more!

Braxy, you are absolutely hilarious. Our friends always say you should have your own television show. We all believe that you should. Your personality is absolutely contagious. You put a smile on each one of our faces daily. Your big brother just adores you. You are your mommy's physical twin. Also, I think your big sister thinks she gave birth to you. She treats you like you are her son or her lifelike doll baby.

After having two kids already, I can't say that raising you has been any kind of struggle. Mommy and I always say that there is nothing you could do that your siblings haven't already done. As your father, I can say adding you to the mix have been trying though. Schedules have become even tighter, finances have been strained at times, but those are both things I'm glad to overcome for you and your siblings.

You three have made me stronger than I have ever been. However, you three are also my biggest weakness. Everyone that knows me knows that if they wanted to hurt me, they just had to get to you. However, they also know there are no lengths I will not go to protect each of you. I hope and pray I am teaching you all lessons that only a father can teach you.

You must all understand you have taught me just as much. I cherish the moments we have spent together, and I look forward to the memories we will make in the future. I promise to love you three as long as I can, as hard as I can. That is a promise that I will keep for as long as I live. I Love My Lil Hennys!

Love Dad,

Brian Henderson

Brian H.

2

CHAPTER TWO

DEAR LYRIC

Dear Lyric J,

I want to first express my gratitude to God, and to you, as my child. It wasn't until I found out you were on the way, that I realized that I was still attempting to control my life. By bringing you in this world, God showed me my life wasn't for me to guide and control, but to live, and remain a student in preparation for what's to come!

Growing up in Danville as you have thus far, I learned a lot. Your Poppa (Grandpa) and Moosie (Grandma) were great parents to me and instilled a set of morals and values as a guide for life. Even with them both being in my life daily, I learned good and bad traits that neither were aware of. I was a good child, but nowhere near perfect. I made good and bad decisions as I grew and molded into the man I am today. The same will go for you. I will give you all the tools I have to help you through your journey, for your journey will be much different than mine. You too will make mistakes as you learn, and I will be there to help you along the way. You will read about some of my mistakes, and hopefully, they will be of assistance when you have questions and need answers in life.

Having a child was something I had always envisioned and planned to do in the perfect controlled environment! I saw husband, wife, and child, as my parents and brothers had done. I was sitting in the backseat of my friend's car when I received the call that your mother was pregnant! After the conversation was over, I began to cry in silence! I was happy and sad at the same time! I was happy to know I was about to be a father, but sad knowing you would have to split your time between me and your mother which is unfair to you! I was 27 years old, but I was still worried what my parents would think, being I'm the only one in my family having a child out of wedlock. That night I prayed and meditated, accepting that I had made a mistake! God revealed to me that night that he takes the mistakes in our lives and creates perfection. You, my child, are perfection!

I began preparing for you immediately! I knew that the well-being of your mother would have a direct correlation with yours. I didn't want her to experience any stress or worry, or it would have an ill effect on you! Our conversations were very pleasant and respectful! I made sure that any discomforts she had, I offered a solution! I felt that by treating her well, you would sense it as well and feel the love too. I attempted to make sure all of her needs were met, as if she was you, because she was carrying you!

When I found out you were going to be a baby girl, it made me reflect over my entire life! A since of fear came over me! I immediately envisioned the manipulator and womanizer I once was, and envisioned you meeting a similar or worse version of me in the future! I again received clarification from God. The only thing I have total control over is the man I become from this day forward! You helped me lose the little bit of the old me that still existed. I wanted to allow you to meet a father, a man that you can trust, believe in, idolize, and look for in the future!

When you were born, I was there for every moment! When they sat you under the light, I wondered if it was too hot for your skin! I ignorantly asked, "How do I go about molding your head to the correct shape?" I didn't know anything, besides you were the most precious gift I had ever received! I allowed you to sleep on my chest, so you could hear and remember my heart beat forever! I practiced swaddling you and making sure you were comfortable! When we took you home, I was so happy and nervous at the same time. I had three weeks to be with you every second of the day. These were three of the best weeks in my life! Your sleep patterns were off, and you were wide awake from 2:00 am to 5:00 am. After your mother would feed you, I would burp you, and walk up and down the hallway with you! I would hold you or sit you in your boppy and have full conversations with you. I would sing and read you poetry throughout the day to you. I was trying my best to maximize every second with you, because I knew I would not have this time forever!

Having to go back to work, back home to Richmond, was the hardest thing I ever had to do! I always envisioned being able to see my child daily, come home to my child and support you! This was the only regret that I had, and I felt like I was failing you! I felt that my duty and purpose as a father could not be done adequately from a far, but I had no other choice!

I would drive to Danville every weekend to be with and spend time with you! I would flood you with positive affirmations! I would let you know how special you were to me, and how special you were going to be to this world! As time would go on, my heart would be broken. You spent the majority of your time with my mom, your grandmother! She loved on you, nurtured, comforted, and became your place of refuge! I wanted so badly for you to want me when you were hungry, sleepy, scared, or during any emotion that you felt! Yet, you would cry for my mom, reach for my mom! I was so jealous and envious, but I knew my time away from you was the cause! This was a testing and hurtful time for me.

As you got a little older and began drinking formula, I was able to bring you to Richmond so we could reconnect and build a bond of our own! You were also able to build a bond with my wife, your pumpkin mom! Seeing you happy and connecting with her was so refreshing and adorable. These were the moments I dreamed of! Being able to feed, change, burp, and put you to sleep without anyone else around to take your attention away!

These moments together brought me so much joy, and a bond that has been so strong ever since! One memory that melted my heart will be embedded in my brain forever was when I came to pick you up from your mom and grandmother. You would not stop crying for them. They had been trying for a while. The moment I came in the room and greeted you, your tears stopped, and you laid your head on my shoulder! They couldn't believe that nothing they tried would work, but my presence alone brought you comfort. They labeled you as daddy's girl that day!

Through the years you have taught me so much! I've watched you grow. I've heard your vocabulary expand, and I have listened to your mocking of my every word and mannerisms. You've helped me remain poised and direct in all my actions, knowing you are watching my every move! You showed me that you are strong and capable of handling every obstacle! You have a blended family, and it is helping you to be well versed. The exposure you gained from being around different families, dynamics, and age groups has advanced you beyond your years, while allowing you to be a care free child. When I do see confusion in your eyes, or hear it in your responses, I'm able to address it therapeutically without your knowing, allowing you to remain in this pure state of mind.

Your mind is so inquisitive, and I love that about you! You force me to continue to learn and grow so I can prepare for your random questions, which are hilarious and cute to me! I love addressing your questions by attacking them immediately! We watch YouTube videos together, learning more about the solar system, earthquakes, tsunamis, and anything that comes to mind! I love how we create our own games to play and spend quality time together talking! I love how you come lay on me when we are watching television together! I never get tired of you touching, hugging, and biting on my cheeks!

Hearing you express for over a year, that you want to live with me until you graduate was the best thing I've ever heard. Yet knowing it is a process that your mother would not be fond of hurts me! I understand her feelings because you are amazing, and she would be in the situation I'm currently in! I want you to know that I will fight for your wants and needs constantly, and whatever the future holds will be the way they're meant to be! I'm already preparing for those questions, even though I know I'm being a great father and support, and everyone else knows! You're still learning what a father is! It's possible that you will still feel a sense of neglect and rejection from me! I will listen closely to your sentiments, and never become defensive, because these will be your true feelings and emotions! I will explain the best way I know how if this occurs in the future! I will be an open book so that you can hopefully avoid placing your children in the same situation your mother and I placed you!

I tell you all the time how much I love you and appreciate you! I always clarify and break down what love really means so you understand it to the fullest! When I say you have given love a brand new meaning in my life, I mean it from my soul. I couldn't have asked God for a better child! You continue to help me evolve daily, and I am forever grateful! You are amazing, and I know you will accomplish things far greater than I could imagine. Always have self-confidence, knowing God has blessed you with the gifts needed for success. Remain humble and always have compassion in your heart for others. Just as happy you are to call me daddy, I'm even happier to call you my daughter! You are seven years old right now, and I look forward to many more years of unlimited blessings from being your father! I love you forever!

Love Your Daddy,

Anthony Hailstock

Anthony H.

3

CHAPTER THREE

DEAR CHILDREN

Dear Children,

To all my children (those present and those yet to arrive), I thank God for sending you to me and for trusting in me to raise you. You were all wanted, and there were no mistakes in your creation, no matter the circumstance. Know that I love each one of you more than I love myself. This may be something impossible to understand until you become a parent yourself.

There is no real way to truly prepare to be a parent. I had to learn by trial in error, while also gaining wisdom from experiences of others. I pray that I have done right by you and made many more correct decisions than errors in your upbringing.

I am not sure what circumstances have you reading this instead of hearing from me directly. I am not sure what I have left to you, but wisdom is what I wish to impart. This world will not be kind to you, and you should not expect to receive mercy from it. We are not like other people; black people are truly unique and our history hidden from us. I hope that I have taught you how to be free and critical thinkers. Make it your life's work to find out about your past from ancient times to even just a few years ago.

I want you to learn where you have been to determine where you should go. The society we live in is very individualistic; this is not our way. True joy and fulfillment comes from helping others and enriching your community. Always honor the Most High, and by doing so, honor your family and yourself. Remember that your conduct is a reflection not just of yourself, but of all of us. What you do to others will always be done to you, and if it fails to visit you, it will visit your children. Honor and uplift your people wherever you go. Be upright and honest, and deal with people fairly, and you will always find success!

To my Daughters,

There is NOTHING inferior about the feminine principles that you embody. You are equal and opposite of any man, the perfect compliment. As your father, I am so proud to have my daughters as you have the deepest parts of me. You are the glue of our families; you will ensure the continuation of us all. Emotional strength and resolution are your inheritance. Your mothers have endured the worse the world could do. Please always remember that when you feel overwhelmed and unsure. Never fall back from that which MUST be done, and always do your best.

Take great care in selecting the man you would marry. He should be loyal, strong, intelligent, kind and focused on others and family. Only **THIS** man will be a good husband and life partner for you. **DO NOT** compromise on this **NO MATTER** what your heart may tell you. If you bend on this, you will waste the best years of your life on foolishness.

If you encounter a man like the one I have described, be his partner. Encourage him, love him, honor him, challenge him, respect him, and believe in him. Find level headed and wise women to connect with to form sisterships with them; you will need each other as life goes on. When children come, take time with them. Time is the most important thing, and when it is gone, there is no way to reclaim it. Remember your sisterhood when they come because you cannot raise children alone. Whatever you desire and purpose to do, do it. Whatever aspirations you have, strive for them. Adopt an entrepreneurial mindset and seek to generate your own income. A good man will not be intimidated but will support you in this.

To my Sons,

Strength and honor are your inheritance and your obligation. There is no glory for you in this society, except when a good woman bestows it upon you. The world you find yourself in will hate you because of your strengths and natural abilities. You are the leader of your family, and your conduct should be above reproach. I am proud of you, and I know that you will bring honor to our name.

You will inherit the strongest parts of me. You must establish yourself and adopt and entrepreneurial mindset in learning to generate your own income. Once you find a wife and have children, all your effort and substance will be for them. It is the duty of a good man to care for his family first, meaning that they will stand on your shoulders and you **MUST** provide a firm foundation for them. They are your crown and glory. A good woman will appreciate and respect you. Find a wife who is loyal, kind, selfless, beautiful, focused on family, and who makes you a better man. Take exceptional care of the one you choose to be your wife, because a foolish woman will destroy you.

Do not make friends with silly and wayward people, those who always seek to do wrong, or engage in things that are vice or immoral. This will make it nearly impossible to be who you need to be for your family. Do not waste your money, energy and life on foolish things. Never shrink back from doing what you must, even if it means your life. Use your physical strength to protect your family and spiritual insights to recognize danger before it comes upon you. Always bring honor to yourself and your family.

When children come, guide them, love them and spend time with them as they are the only way you can remain in the earth. They are a blessing always and never a hindrance. Form friendships with good and honorable men that you can trust and support each other, as you will need their support as the year's progress. Seek to do right and be kind to people always.

My words are the most important things I can leave you. Know that I love each of you deeply. Stay together, and love and support each other. Spend time with each other and endure life together. Help each other with your children and raise your children together. Make **SURE** you all understand history so that you will not be fooled by the lies that permeate this world. Never forget what our people have endured to bring us to this point. Never turn your back on our people and our history. Take us all forward! We live in you now, and wherever you go, you take us with you. Look to the Most High, and model yourselves accordingly. If you do this, you will establish our family forever. I believe in all of you. Know that anything is possible. May you all inherit the best parts of me!

Love Daddy!!!!

Jamal Hasan

J. I. Hasan

4

CHAPTER FOUR

DEAR SKYY AND MORGAN

Dear Skyy and Morgan,

On this day, I stand extremely proud of you two for learning how to read and interpret what I have prepared for you. First, I want to thank you **BOTH** for allowing me to be your father and experience "family" in an even greater way.

My purpose of this letter is to give you the truth about your father, so you won't have to go to anyone else for it.

See your daddy never really knew your grandfather, until I was much older. Your granny wanted to protect me as a child from the ugly parts of this world, so she didn't always tell me both sides of my dad. You didn't get to meet him before he passed.

Your grandfather was a very intellectual, successful, and cool guy. He was a Navy Veteran and worked at the Southern Virginia Mental Health Institute, among other positions. However, he also had troubles with alcohol, tobacco, and drug addictions. Like many of us, he had some issues. In this life, no one is immune to making mistakes, and it's very important to me that you understand this as soon as possible. With that being said, I will be honest with you about myself, so you too can be confident and proud of who you are and where you come from.

Your father was the youngest born of three boys. I had to take many losses since I was seven years old, but I also kept on striving to win. At home, I lived with your granny and uncles, Jay Jay and Kevin. They were teenagers by the time I was seven. Unfortunately, my oldest brother, your uncle Jay Jay, was fatally shot and killed outside of our home in Danville, Virginia at his age of twenty years old.

As you can imagine, this loss hurt me as a kid, and to deal with the pain, I just ignored it. I put it in the back of my mind and kept on living my life. Your father may have been a lot of things, but I was not a quitter. I always did well in school and tried my best to make good grades. I also purposefully tried staying away from fighting to make my mom and brothers proud. I didn't have a lot of money growing up, so when I was old enough I began working at Food Lion bagging groceries. Then, I went to Finishline where I sold sneakers and apparel. To help cope with the pain of losing a brother and not spending time with my father, I also got involved in sports. I enjoyed baseball, basketball, and track, but the sport I loved most was football. I was a leader on the field at little league, high school, and college level. However, I was not perfect either.

Your father enjoyed hanging out late past curfew, chasing girls, and being cool with what parents call, the "wrong crowd." I honestly was searching for ways to escape reality and tried smoking and drinking based on negative influencers and curiosity. I never went too far with anything though. I was always told too much of anything is bad for you. Eventually, I found ways to use all of my emotions and pain to fuel my talents. However, that very same pain and emotion would cause me to hate myself. I didn't love the things that made me Travis and did not want the life that was given to me; the good and/or the bad.

So, while in college my grandmother, your great grandmother, passed away from diabetes and I really felt alone. I wanted to give up on everything that I worked so hard to accomplish. She was a major support for my success and I became depressed. I had graduated high school in 2003, was attending Virginia State University, walked on to their football team, eventually earned an athletic scholarship, and I was ready to give it all up.

Then someone came along at the perfect time. It was 2006 when I met Shana, your mom, in business finance class. She was smart, unique and gave off a very relaxed vibe whenever she was around. We could be ourselves around each other and tell each other our deepest and darkest secrets. We both fell in love with one another, but not like in the Disney movies with a prince, crowns, or a shining chariot.

We both had prior relationships and had to make a choice; be serious with one another or continue to play the dating game. We chose to be with one another but the road got rougher before it got smoother. We learned from our relationship that, "If you love someone, then wait on them if you want to, but never be anyone's fool."

True love always prevails and we both graduated college with Bachelor's degrees in Business Management, but the world was going through a recession. Jobs were scarce. At times we had no place to live, not a lot of money, only one vehicle, no food, but we had each other's love. Eventually, I landed a salary paying job as a Youth Counselor. Your mom gained employment at Virginia Commonwealth University and Virginia State University in the financial aid and student resource departments.

Over those years of being in a serious relationship, your mom helped me heal from the pain I ignored for so many years. She did all this and we weren't even married yet. We wanted to be married before having children, but we had debts and things don't always go as planned. Just when I saw how great this life was, your mom blessed me with an even greater gift. She told me that we were having our first child, and eventually, Skyy was born.

Skyy, you were 6 months old when your mother and father got married. Your presence taught me to value myself just as I valued you. I focused and dedicated so much time to you that I gave up my first love of football, to be with you more. At the time, I played running back and was #19 for the Richmond Revolution, a new Indoor Football Team of the Indoor Football League in 2010. However, I wanted to be your father more than a football player.

Life progressed, and you were four years old, and here comes Morgan. Morgan, you were the total opposite of Skyy, and I had to rethink all that I thought I knew about parenting. You taught me a very important aspect of life. You taught me to accept people for who they genuinely are, whether you like them or not. You wanted and loved your mommy as a baby so much that I couldn't spend as much time with you like I did with Skyy. Your mom breast fed you both so I understood the bond established, but I wanted to prove my love too. I was hurting again, but you finally outgrew that "nook" and now you will not leave me alone at all. You make me very happy!

In closing, you girls are five and nine years old when I wrote this. I believe this is just what you will need at a time in your lives when you start asking yourself questions like, “Who am I? Where do I come from?” I hope I did a good enough job as your father. I pray you are as proud of me as I have been of you both, since the day you were born.

Love Papi!!!

Travis Valentine

Travis V

5

CHAPTER FIVE

DEAR BRANSON

I was an eighteen year old student-athlete at Hampton University, when I received the call about becoming your father. I was afraid, nervous, and I had many doubts. I didn't know how to be a father and I didn't know what to expect. However, May 9, 2006 came and my life changed forever!

Less than two weeks prior to your birth, I had just finished my first year of college and I had just turned nineteen. I was still a young man and had a lot of growing to do myself. The first time I held you, I was overwhelmed with joy as I stared at my almost ten pound baby-boy. The first couple of years were stressful because of immature behaviors between your mother and me. While we had our own struggles during those times, much like today, you were a great kid and always made us proud.

As you got older, I took extreme pleasure watching you grow and go through your different stages of life. You went from being a bucking bull rider to playing soccer, playing baseball, playing basketball, and you even gave football one good season. I must say, as a father, it is beautiful to see a lot of myself in you as an athlete; though I feel you will be better than me when it's all said and done.

I thank God for your mother. While she hasn't been the easiest to deal with, I must say she has always put you first. She has always acknowledged my love for you as your father and that I try to be the best example I can for you. At times, I wasn't always able to support you financially. There were also plenty of times that I wasn't the best example or father I could be. However, she was still patient and understanding. As you grew older, you were able to talk and let me know the things you needed more from me.

When you gained your voice that was the turning point in my life as a father. I remember when I was getting ready to go overseas to play basketball. You were with me and the family at my going away cookout. My best-friend stopped by to visit and asked if I wanted to ride to the store with him. I told you that, "I would be right back." However, I will never forget your response. You looked at me with so much hurt in your eyes. You cried out and said, “You’re always leaving me.” After hearing that from you, I couldn’t go to the store that evening. I wanted to be with you!

Even when I left to go pursue my dream, that conversation was forever stuck in my mind and heart. Every time we spoke on Skype, I saw that hurt kid. So after I came home after the first season, when it was time for me to go back, I turned down my next contract. I decided to come home and be that father I promised myself I would be for you.

Not only did we spend more time together, but I went back to school to finish my degree. You were my motivation to better myself. Now I have a good job and just bought my first house. The best house-warming gift came when you decided to live with me and made it our house. I thank God for seeing me as a scared teenage boy, who needed a son to change him into a man. You are that gift from God who helped me grow and I will forever be grateful to you.

I'm still growing and I'm still learning, but I must say you're my biggest blessing.

I Love You Son!!!

Demario Mattox

Demario M.

Thank You

for allowing us

to be your

Fathers!

Letters

From Your

Fathers

Things We Want You to Know

Volume Two

Coming Soon!!!

Made in the USA
Monee, IL
01 March 2020

22283567R00046